MAURITANIA 2016 HUMAN RIGHTS REPORT

EXECUTIVE SUMMARY

Mauritania is a highly centralized Islamic Republic with a president as head of state and a constitution grounded in French civil law and sharia (Islamic law). The Senate and National Assembly exercise legislative functions but were weak relative to the executive. Voters elect municipal councilors, who, in turn, elect senators. Voters reelected President Mohamed Ould Abdel Aziz to a second and final five-year term in 2014. In 2013 Union for the Republic (UPR), the president's party, won 76 of 147 seats in the National Assembly in direct legislative elections, which some opposition parties boycotted. Several political parties, but not the major opposition parties, agreed in late October to hold a referendum on proposed amendments to the constitution, but it had not taken place by year's end.

Civilian authorities maintained effective control over the security forces.

The chief human rights problems were use of torture by law enforcements officers; arbitrary arrests; holding individuals in lengthy pretrial and incommunicado detention; harsh, overcrowded, and dangerous prison conditions; continuing slavery and slavery-related practices; and, trafficking in persons. Violations of freedom of the press, association, and conscience were also of serious concern.

Other human rights problems included incarceration of children with adult prisoners; government influence over the judiciary; arbitrary limits on freedom of assembly; public corruption; and restrictions on religious freedom. By law only Muslims may be citizens. Other reported human rights abuses included gender-based violence against women and girls; discrimination against women; female genital mutilation/cutting (FGM/C); early and forced marriage; political marginalization of sub-Saharan (non-Arab) ethnic groups and of the Haratine caste of slave descendants; racial and ethnic discrimination; discrimination against lesbian, gay, bisexual, transgender, and intersex (LGBTI) persons and persons with HIV/AIDS; child labor; and, inadequate and selective arbitrary enforcement of laws, including labor laws.

The government took modest steps to punish officials who committed violations and prosecuted a number of violators, but officials frequently acted with impunity. Civil society organizations objected to the scant number of indictments handed down by the authorities.

Section 1. Respect for the Integrity of the Person, Including Freedom from:

a. Arbitrary Deprivation of Life and Other Unlawful or Politically Motivated Killings

There were no reports the government or its agents committed arbitrary or unlawful killings.

b. Disappearance

There were no reports of politically motivated disappearances.

c. Torture and Other Cruel, Inhuman, or Degrading Treatment or Punishment

The constitution and law prohibit torture, but nongovernmental organizations (NGOs) reported security and law enforcement officials tortured their members. Methods of abuse reportedly included beatings, stripping of clothing, and denial of food. There were credible reports of torture, beatings, and abuse in police detention centers and several prisons throughout the country, and in gendarmerie and military facilities. Defendants reported that police took them to the beach, partially buried them, and subjected to mock executions. Other defendants testified in court they were beaten, or tied to chairs for days at a time.

In August 2015 the government adopted a law against torture that requires the establishment of a mechanism for its prevention. This law considers torture, acts of torture, and inhuman or degrading punishments as crimes against humanity not subject to a statute of limitations. The law specifically covers activities in prisons, rehabilitation centers for minors in conflict with the law, places of custody, psychiatric institutions, detention centers, areas of transit, and border crossing points.

In April the government created the National Mechanism for Prevention of Torture (MNP) as an independent governmental body charged with investigating credible allegations of torture. The MNP had not launched any investigation by year's end.

On August 9, the Initiative for the Resurgence of the Abolitionist Movement (IRA), an active antislavery and "Haratine rights" NGO, reported that 13 of its members were tortured. These individuals were arrested and convicted in connection with a June 29 riot in Nouakchott in which several police officers were injured. The IRA complained that authorities arrested and held these activists incommunicado for nearly two weeks, the maximum allowable period of such detention under antiterrorism legislation. The IRA also stated that their activists were regularly tortured and humiliated while in police custody. Some IRA defendants testified they were not tortured, while others said they were tortured and named their alleged torturers. At their August 3 trial, Moussad Ould Bilal Ould Biram, the first defendant interrogated, said that he was tortured badly. Abdellahi Ould Maatallah, the next defendant to testify, also recounted being beaten and insulted. The arrests took place during Ramadan, and many defendants complained that police failed to feed them after sunset ended the day's requirement to fast. The defendants, their lawyers, and several other IRA members said they repeatedly drew the attention of authorities and the MNP to these alleged abuses without any reaction from the prison administration, the MNP, or the prosecutor.

On December 7, the news website *al-Akhbar* reported child detainees in the Central Prison of Nouakchott were regularly tortured. Prison authorities denied the allegation.

On February 2, the news website *Cridem* reported that the UN Rapporteur on Torture, and Other Cruel, Inhuman or Degrading Treatments, at the end of a 10-day visit to the country, asked authorities to implement existing laws and protect suspects and detainees from torture and ill treatment. *Cridem* also reported the UN rapporteur stated that some prisoners, specifically Salafist terrorists, were tortured, but authorities did not conduct any investigation of these allegations.

The United Nations reported that in the year to December 20, it received two allegations of sexual exploitation and abuse against Mauritanian peacekeepers for incidents that allegedly occurred during the year. The allegations involved personnel deployed to the United Nations Multidimensional Integrated Stabilization Mission in the Central African Republic. According to the United Nations, both allegations were pending investigation by the United Nations and the Mauritanian government at year's end.

Prison and Detention Center Conditions

Prison conditions were harsh and life threatening. Prison authorities kept a mixed population of prisoners in prison facilities throughout the country regardless of their sentences. They held convicted prisoners with pretrial detainees in the same facilities. Drugs were often trafficked among prisoners, which the government acknowledged was caused by lax security for visitors. Prisoners often rebelled and disobeyed authorities in protest against violence and inhumane treatment meted out by jailers. Poor security conditions and dangerous inmates sharing cells with less dangerous ones obliged prisoners to live in a climate of violence, and some had to pay bribes to other prisoners to avoid brutalization and harassment. Human rights groups continued to report prisons were overcrowded and lacked adequate sanitation and medical facilities.

Physical Conditions: The Mauritanian Observatory for Human Rights reported in 2015 that there were seven main prisons, four in Nouakchott and three in the interior. It continued to denounce the poor conditions of these prisons. There were two separate prisons for women, one in the capital, Nouakchott, and the other in the second largest city, Nouadhibou. Most supervisors were men; there was a severe shortage of female supervisors. Male guards provided security at women's prisons because the all-male National Guard was assigned this task nationwide. There were some women supervisors in prisons, but they were not from the National Guard. An Italian NGO operated a detention center for minors, the only facility that came close to meeting international standards. These prisons were in addition to detention centers located in police stations throughout the country.

Prisons remained overcrowded. For example, Dar Naim Prison, the main civil prison in Nouakchott, had a capacity of 300 inmates but held 595, of whom 239 were convicted prisoners and 356, pretrial detainees. Authorities frequently held pretrial detainees with convicted and often dangerous prisoners. Male guards frequently monitored female inmates in the women's prison of Nouakchott, a practice criticized by the National Commission on Human Rights (CNDH). Conditions of detention for women were generally better than for men. According to prison officials, the women's prison in Nouakchott was less crowded.

The Salah ad Dine Prison, the maximum-security facility in Adrar, remained open and held incommunicado a number of inmates convicted of terrorism related offenses.

Due to deteriorating conditions, authorities closed the juvenile detention facility at Beila and transferred 62 children between the ages of 15 and 17 to Nouakchott's Central Prison and 15 to the prison in Nouadhibou. The minors had contact with adult prisoners, including those convicted of terrorist offenses and other violent crimes. The Ministry of Justice sometimes gave temporary custody of the children of prisoners to another family member to remove them from confinement.

Authorities reported seven inmate deaths during the year. The cause of death of two of the seven inmates was infectious diseases. Upon the death of an inmate in custody, the family of the deceased has the right to request an autopsy. During the year, only one family member asked for an autopsy. The result showed death was due to natural causes.

According to the Mauritanian Observatory for Human Rights, access to food for most prisoners was generally inadequate, as were sanitary conditions in prison kitchens. Medical facilities and staff were similarly inadequate, particularly in the Dar Naim men's prison and at the Central Prison. The government allocated a budget of 600 ouguiyas ($1.71) a day for each prisoner for food and medical supplies. Generalized corruption in the prison system, smuggling of medicines, and lack of skilled medical staff accounted for most deficiencies. Ventilation, lighting, and potable water in many cells and holding areas ranged from inadequate to nonexistent.

Administration: Efforts to improve recordkeeping continued to progress slowly. Local NGOs reported prison officials often misplaced prisoner files, leading in some cases to postponement of release. In January prisoners who had completed their sentences rioted at Nouakchott Central Prison after authorities failed to honor their scheduled release dates.

Independent prison ombudsmen did not exist, but authorities permitted prisoners to file allegations of abuse with the CNDH. Regulations also allowed inmates to choose one of their own to represent them in dealings with the administration, and prisoners occasionally made use of this opportunity.

Effective May 1, the previously weekly visits by imams to prisoners increased to three visits a week, and every week the Penitentiary Administration chose an imam to conduct the Friday prayer in all prisons.

The government acknowledged the allegations regarding inhumane conditions but rarely took corrective action.

Independent Monitoring: The government permitted prison and detention center visits by NGOs, diplomats, and international human rights observers. The International Committee of the Red Cross (ICRC) had unlimited access to prisons and conducted multiple visits, including visits to terrorism suspects. The ICRC worked with prison authorities to improve conditions of detention and the treatment of inmates by renovating infrastructure and providing food, medical assistance, water, sanitation, prison management advice, and legal safeguards through protection of prisoners' rights and contact with their families. The ICRC conducted frequent visits to the Dar Naim, the Central Prison in Nouakchott, and to prisons in Aleg, Selibaby, and Kaedi. Corrections officials continued to allow access to several prisons in Nouakchott to diplomatic personnel, who had the opportunity to interview prisoners and staff members.

Improvements: In August the ICRC renovated and equipped the prison in Kaedi. The NGO Noura Foundation conducted sanitation and hygienic training in the prisons of Nouakchott and Aleg. Caritas Mauritania opened a library in the Dar Naim Prison to enable prisoners to access reading materials. It also implemented an awareness program to fight the transmission of infectious diseases such as HIV/AIDS, malaria, and tuberculosis.

The Ministry of Justice undertook several measures to improve conditions and reduce overcrowding, including the deportation of foreign prisoners to their home countries, pardons, commutation of sentences, or conditional release of prisoners convicted of minor crimes. Prison officials held female prisoners in Nouadhibou in a separate facility within the walls of the main prison.

d. Arbitrary Arrest or Detention

The constitution and law prohibit arbitrary arrest and detention, but authorities did not observe these prohibitions. In some cases, authorities arbitrarily arrested and detained protesters, human rights activists, and journalists (see section 2.a.).

Role of the Police and Security Apparatus

Under the Ministry of Interior and Decentralization, the National Police is responsible for enforcing the law and maintaining order in urban areas. The National Guard, under the same ministry, performs limited police functions in keeping with its peacetime role as the guarantor of physical security at government facilities, including prisons. For instance, regional authorities may call upon it to restore civil order during riots and other large-scale disturbances. The gendarmerie, a specialized paramilitary organization under the Ministry of Defense, is responsible for maintaining civil order around metropolitan areas and providing law enforcement services in rural areas. The Ministry of Interior and Decentralization's newest police force, the General Group for Road Safety, maintains security on roads and operates checkpoints throughout the country.

Police and gendarmes were poorly paid, trained, and equipped. Corruption and impunity were serious problems. Police and gendarmes reportedly regularly sought bribes at nightly roadblocks in Nouakchott and at checkpoints between cities. There were numerous reports police at such roadblocks arbitrarily detained individuals, often without probable cause, for several hours or overnight.

Arrest Procedures and Treatment of Detainees

The law requires duly authorized arrest warrants, although their issuance was uncommon. Authorities generally did not inform detainees of the accusations against them until the conclusion of an investigation. The law requires that in most cases courts review the legality of a person's detention within 48 hours of arrest, but police may extend the period for an additional 48 hours, and a prosecutor or court may detain persons for up to an additional 15 days in national terrorism cases. Authorities generally respected the two-week deadline for formally arraigning or releasing terrorism suspects in national security cases. Only after the prosecutor submits charges does a suspect have the right to contact an attorney. By law indigent defendants are entitled to an attorney at state expense, but frequently either legal representation was unavailable or attorneys did not speak a defendant's language. There was a bail system, but judges sometimes refused such requests arbitrarily or set inordinately high bail.

Arbitrary Arrest: There were cases of arbitrary arrest and detention of journalists (see section 2.a.). Police arrested a number of human right activists and journalists without charge or hearings.

Pretrial Detention: Lengthy pretrial detention was a problem, although no statistics on the average length of detention were available. Security force members sometimes arrested demonstrators and held them longer than regulations allow, often due to lack of capacity to process cases in a timely manner, or to obtain confessions. By law authorities may hold a minor for no more than six months while the detainee awaits trial. Nevertheless, there were reports many individuals, including minors, remained in pretrial detention for excessively long periods due to judicial inefficiency.

Detainee's Ability to Challenge Lawfulness of Detention before a Court: A detainee has ability to challenge lawfulness of his or her detention before a court under two circumstances. If a person remains arrested after the end of his/her legal period of detention, the detainee has the right to complain before a court against the administration of the prison or the penitential authority that arrested the detainee. Secondly, if the detainee disagrees with his/her sentence, he or she has the right to call for an appeal before a court of appeal or the Supreme Court.

e. Denial of Fair Public Trial

The constitution and law provide for an independent judiciary, but the judiciary was not autonomous. The executive branch continued to exercise significant influence over the judiciary through its ability to appoint and remove judges. Observers often perceived many judges to be corrupt and unskilled.

Trial Procedures

The law provides for due process, and defendants enjoy a presumption of innocence. The law requires that authorities inform defendants of the charges against them, but the government did not normally respect this provision. Defendants did not often learn of the charges until the investigation was complete. Authorities generally provided defendants with free interpretation as required; however, the quality of these services was generally poor. Defendants have the right to a fair and public trial. They also have the right to be present during trial. All defendants, including the indigent, have the right to legal counsel, but authorities rarely respected this right. Likewise, defendants may confront or question witnesses and present witnesses and evidence in both civil and criminal cases. Defendants have the right to access government held evidence, although in practice it was difficult to obtain such evidence. Defendants generally had adequate time and facilities to prepare their defense. Defendants enjoy the right not to be compelled to testify or confess guilt and have the right of appeal. These rights extend to minorities and men but do not extend equally to women. Court proceedings are by law conducted in Arabic, and interpreters are not always available for those defendants who do not understand that language. Some bilingual judges speak with defendants in French.

Sharia is, in part, the basis for law and court procedures. Courts did not treat women equally with men in all cases.

A special court hears cases involving persons under age 18. Children who appeared before the court received more lenient sentences than adults did, and extenuating circumstances received greater consideration. The minimum age for a child to stand trial is 12 years. Juvenile offenders between ages 12 and 17 generally served sentences at detention centers for minors, although several NGOs expressed concern regarding the holding of youthful offenders in the general population, including with more dangerous inmates, at Nouakchott Central Prison.

On August 3, the trial began of 23 men charged in connection with a June 29 riot in Nouakchott during which several police officers were injured. On August 23, local press reported that the EU delegation in the country described the rumored verdict as severe, and the UN High Commissioner for Human Rights said the trial was riddled with irregularities, a charge denied by the public prosecutor.

Political Prisoners and Detainees

On August 18, the criminal court of Nouakchott sentenced 13 members of the IRA to sentences ranging from three to 15 years' imprisonment. The court convicted them of leading an unarmed rebellion, violence against police officers, armed assembly, and membership in an unregistered organization. They were widely considered political prisoners, as the court sentenced some purely for membership in an unregistered organization. Some others were shown during the trial to have been present at the riot, but had not directed or participated in the violence. The court convicted and sentenced others for involvement in the riot, although the trial showed they were not present at the riot. Authorities also charged 10 non-IRA members in connection with the riot. The court convicted seven, and acquitted and released three.

Civil Judicial Procedures and Remedies

Complaints of human rights violations fall within the jurisdiction of the Administrative Court. Individuals or organizations may appeal decisions to international regional courts. NGO representatives stated they collaborated with the Administrative Court, but added it was not impartial. There are administrative remedies through the social chamber of the Court of Appeals and the Supreme Court. Persons may sue at the Administrative Court and appeal to the Court of Appeals and then to the Supreme Court.

Property Restitution

Real property ownership in the southern regions has been controversial since the government expelled tens of thousands of non-Arab sub-Saharans from communities based in the Senegal River Valley (Halpulaar, Soninke, and Wolof) from 1989 to 1991 amid tensions with neighboring Senegal. Many non-Arabs were dispossessed of their land, which regional officials subsequently sold or ceded to Beydane ("Arabo-Berbers" or "White Moors" (see section 6, National/Racial/Ethnic Minorities). Although the government continued to make modest efforts to indemnify returning deportees, it did not fully restore their property rights. The government reimbursed some in cash, and provided jobs for others.

f. Arbitrary or Unlawful Interference with Privacy, Family, Home, or Correspondence

The constitution prohibits such actions, and there were no reports the government failed to respect these prohibitions.

Section 2. Respect for Civil Liberties, Including:

a. Freedom of Speech and Press

The constitution provides for freedom of speech and press, and the government generally respected these rights; however, it sometimes arbitrarily and selectively applied regulations to suppress individuals or groups of individuals who oppose government policies. Individuals were generally free to criticize the government publicly or privately but were occasionally subject to retaliation. The constitution and law prohibit racial or ethnic propaganda. The government has used these provisions against political opponents, accusing them of "racism" or "promoting national disunity" for speaking out against the extreme underrepresentation in government of Haratines and sub-Saharan Africans.

Press and Media Freedoms: The government owned two daily newspapers and most broadcast media; five radio stations and five television stations were independent. Several independent daily publications generally expressed a wide variety of views with limited restrictions. Throughout the year, incidents of government retaliation against media deemed too outspoken increased.

For example, on April 16, *Deyloul* (a news website close to the opposition) reported two journalists (Jedna Deida of *Mauriweb* and Babacar N'Diaye of *Cridem* news websites) were tried on April 15. They were arrested and then released following a complaint for defamation filed by the eldest son of President Aziz.

Independent media remained the principal source of information for most citizens, followed by government media. Government media focused primarily on official news but provided some coverage of opposition activities and views.

<u>Violence and Harassment</u>: There were several reported incidents of violence against and harassment of journalists. On January 27, the president of the country's journalist syndicate, Moctar Salem, stated during a television broadcast that 12 journalists faced complaints filed by various government officials with the Ministry of Justice--a tactic used by the government to intimidate journalists.

For example, on January 25, Sidi Ali Ould Belemech, a journalist with the *Mourassiloun* news website, was detained and questioned by police after Ministry of Finance official filed a complaint against Belemech for criticizing him.

<u>Censorship or Content Restrictions</u>: Some opposition leaders asserted they had no effective access to official media. The government made payment of back taxes, at times unpaid for years with official complicity, a matter of priority, threatening the solvency of several independent stations.

On February 15, the Wali (provincial governor) of Hodh El Chargui Region prevented a press crew from the Essirage news group from completing interviews with some communities that were in conflict over a well. The crew allegedly lacked formal authorization from authorities in Nouakchott.

In February the government notified all private media outlets of a temporary suspension of all government funded subscription services and commercial advertising, which had provided financial support to private media. The government stated it planned to use the six billion ouguiyas ($17 million) typically spent annually on media subscriptions and advertising to more equitably support private media. Because of the suspension, however, the private media struggled to survive. On September 18, private media around the country organized a "Day without Press" to protest the government's subscription and advertising suspension, which remained in place at year's end. This was the country's first media strike since 1991.

Some journalists practiced self-censorship when covering topics deemed sensitive, including the military, corruption, and the application of sharia, and there were reports police detained and questioned journalists in connection with their coverage of those topics as well as of slavery.

Internet Freedom

The government did not restrict or disrupt access to the internet or censor online content, and there were no credible reports that the government monitored private online communications without appropriate legal authority. According to the International Telecommunication Union, in 2015 approximately 15 percent of the population used the internet.

The parliament adopted a bill on cybercrime in December 2015 that establishes protection of systems and data. Journalists alleged the legislation would permit authorities to prosecute them for almost anything published online. The legislation would also bring encryption technology under heavy state regulation, and nullify previous laws extending protections to journalists using digital technologies.

Academic Freedom and Cultural Events

There were no reported government restrictions on academic freedom or cultural events.

b. Freedom of Peaceful Assembly and Association

Freedom of Assembly

The constitution provides for freedom of assembly. Registered political parties are not required to seek permission to hold meetings or demonstrations. The law requires NGO organizers to apply to the local administrative chief for permission to hold large meetings or assemblies. Authorities usually granted permission but on some occasions denied it in circumstances that suggested the application of political criteria.

On several occasions, officials with the IRA and other organizations reported security force members arrested their activists for failing to obtain the local prefect's permission to hold a rally.

Freedom of Association

The law provides for freedom of association, and the government generally, but not in every instance, respected this right.

All local NGOs must register with the Ministry of Interior and Decentralization. Generally, if the ministry fails to respond within 45 days to a request to establish an NGO, the NGO may proceed with its work, although it was not considered officially registered.

On August 2, the newspaper *Calame* reported police closed the office of the Progressive Forces for Change, previously the African Liberation Forces of Mauritania, for unauthorized activities.

The government encouraged locally registered NGOs to join the government sponsored Civil Society Platform. Approximately 7,000 local NGOs did so. IRA Mauritania, whose president challenged President Aziz in the 2014 presidential election, has been awaiting official recognition since 2008. Other similar organizations have received government permission to operate. In August a court sentenced 13 IRA members to three to 15 years' imprisonment for their membership in the unregistered organization and participating in a Nouakchott riot on June 29. President Aziz has publicly stated more than once that IRA has never applied for recognition, a claim denied by the IRA vice president.

c. Freedom of Religion

See the Department of State's *International Religious Freedom Report* at www.state.gov/religiousfreedomreport/.

d. Freedom of Movement, Internally Displaced Persons, Protection of Refugees, and Stateless Persons

The constitution and law provide for freedom of internal movement, foreign travel, emigration, and repatriation. The government generally respected these rights, but there were exceptions.

The government cooperated with the Office of the UN High Commissioner for Refugees (UNHCR) and other humanitarian organizations in providing protection and assistance to internally displaced persons, refugees, returning refugees, asylum seekers, stateless persons, vulnerable migrants, or other persons of concern. Resources provided by the government were inadequate to meet the assistance needs of these populations.

<u>In-country Movement</u>: Persons lacking identity cards could not travel freely in some regions. As in previous years, the government set up mobile roadblocks where gendarmes, police, or customs officials checked the papers of travelers.

<u>Exile</u>: The law does not provide for forced exile. Nevertheless, several prominent opponents of the president have remained in self-imposed exile for years for fear of persecution or retaliation.

Ewlad Blad, a popular rap group, representing the country's three largest ethnic groups (Moor/Beydane, Moor/Haratine, and Sub-Saharan/Halpulaar), remained in self-imposed exile in Senegal for fear of prosecution. Their lyrics revolve around social justice, inequality, rising food prices, high levels of corruption, nepotism, and what the group describes as the authoritarian manner of the president at the root of the country's increasing social tensions.

<u>Emigration and Repatriation</u>: Launched in 2013, the National Agency for the Fight against the Vestiges of Slavery, Reintegration, and the Fight against Poverty (Tadamoun) is responsible for overseeing the reintegration of repatriated refugees and providing administration and identification support, as well as for contributing to the social and economic development of resettlement areas. Despite challenges--including food insecurity, land disputes, and inadequate sanitation, health, education, and infrastructure--the government made modest progress in reintegrating repatriated refugees.

Protection of Refugees

<u>Access to Asylum</u>: The law provides for granting of asylum or refugee status, and the government has established a system for providing protection to refugees. UNHCR carries out refugee status determinations under its mandate and then presents cases to the National Consultative Commission for Refugees for recognition.

In accordance with agreements with the Economic Community of West African States on freedom of movement, the government allows West Africans to remain in the country for up to three months, after which they must apply for residency or work permits. Migrants determined to be illegally seeking to reach Spain's nearby Canary Islands were deported.

Stateless Persons

The law allows children born outside the country to Mauritanian mothers and foreign men to obtain Mauritanian nationality at age 17. According to article 15 of the Mauritanian Code of Nationality, as amended, children born to Mauritanian fathers and foreign mothers are automatically Mauritanian. If the father is stateless, children born outside the country are subject to statelessness until age 17, at which point the child is eligible for nationality. The unwillingness of local authorities to process thousands of sub-Saharan Africans who returned from Senegal, following their mass expulsion between 1989 and 1991, rendered the returnees stateless.

Section 3. Freedom to Participate in the Political Process

The constitution provides citizens the ability to choose their government in free and fair periodic elections based on universal and equal suffrage, and conducted by secret ballot.

Elections and Political Participation

Recent Elections: In June 2014 President Aziz won reelection to a second and final five-year term with approximately 82 percent of the vote. Although some opposition groups alleged procedural irregularities and inconsistent application of vote counting policies, the Constitutional Council and international observers endorsed the results of the election.

In 2013 the president's party, the UPR, won 76 of 147 seats in the National Assembly in direct legislative elections, which some opposition parties boycotted.

Voters last elected members of the Senate in 2006. New elections to choose two thirds of the Senate were to have occurred in 2011 but were indefinitely postponed.

On February 11, the Constitutional Council invalidated a government decree calling for renewal of two-thirds of the Senate as unconstitutional. Instead, the council ordered the government to hold elections for the entire senate.

In a May 3 speech, President Aziz announced his intent to dissolve the Senate and replace it with regional councils to focus on development. Such action would require constitutional amendment to abolish the senate and replace it with an indirectly elected body.

<u>Political Parties and Political Participation</u>: The government often favored individuals based on political ties.

The Beydane (Arabs) account for at most 30 percent of the population but occupied about 80 percent of top leadership positions. Haratines (Arab slave descendants) constitute at least 45 percent of the population but held less than 10 percent of the positions. The sub-Saharan ethnic groups (Halpulaar, Soninke, and Wolof) make up about 25 percent of the population and account for less than 10 percent of top leadership positions.

<u>Participation of Women and Minorities</u>: No laws limit the participation of women and minorities in the political process, and women and minorities did so. The law reserves at least 20 seats in the National Assembly for women. Following the 2013 legislative elections, 31 women held seats in the 147-member National Assembly. Of the country's 29 ministers, eight were women, three were Haratines, and six were from non-Arab, sub-Saharan ethnic groups.

Section 4. Corruption and Lack of Transparency in Government

The law provides criminal penalties for official corruption, but authorities did not enforce the law effectively, and officials often engage in corrupt practices with impunity. Corrupt practices were widely believed to exist at all levels of government. The World Bank's most recent Worldwide Governance Indicators reflected that corruption was rampant.

<u>Corruption</u>: Corruption and impunity were serious problems in the public administration, and the government rarely held officials accountable or prosecuted them for abuses. There were reports government officials frequently used their power to obtain favors such as unauthorized exemption from taxes, special grants of land, and preferential treatment during bidding on government projects. Corruption was most pervasive in government procurement but also common in the distribution of official documents, fishing and mining licenses, land, bank loans, and tax payments. Although there was a slight increase in prosecutions for corruption during the year, authorities rarely jailed those found guilty. Instead, they were usually required only to return the funds in question.

On May 27, the Criminal Division for Economic and Financial Crimes arrested Jemila Mint Mohamed, a government employed accountant for project "VAINCRE," a French-funded development project. Authorities charged her with embezzling 700 million ouguiyas ($2 million) from the project, but released her on bail.

In 2015 authorities arrested 32 employees of the state treasury for fraud and the embezzlement of more than one billion ouguiyas ($2.8 million) and dismissed many financial auditors who overlooked the embezzlement in regional treasury services. The embezzlement network extended to the fishing, foreign customs, and health sectors, and led the minister of finance to resign. In August the court convicted 12 of the 32 and sentenced them to two to three years' imprisonment. Investigation for the remaining 20 was ongoing and they remained in detention awaiting trial.

The 2015 anticorruption law was unevenly enforced and mostly used as a weapon against opponents of the regime. The law defines corruption as "all exploitation by a public agent of his position for personal purposes, whether this agent is elected, or in an administrative or judicial position."

Financial Disclosure: The government enforced the requirement that senior officials, including the president, file a declaration of their personal assets at the beginning and end of their service. The information is not available to the public. The last public accounting of President Aziz's personal assets took place in 2010; the president of the Supreme Court declared Aziz did not have to renew the public declaration when he was reelected in 2014. Members of his first administration who resigned in the wake of his reelection had not declared their assets.

Public Access to Information: The law provides for public access to government information, and the government generally granted some access to citizens and noncitizens, including foreign media. The government did not fully implement the law, since the law still requires adoption of implementing legislation before it can take effect.

Section 5. Governmental Attitude Regarding International and Nongovernmental Investigation of Alleged Violations of Human Rights

Several domestic and international human rights groups generally operated without government restriction, investigating and publishing their findings on human rights cases. Government officials were somewhat cooperative and responsive to their views.

<u>Government Human Rights Bodies</u>: The Commissariat for Human Rights and Humanitarian Action designs, promotes, and implements national human rights policies. During the year its budget increased to 595 million ouguiyas ($1.7 million), a 20 million ouguiyas ($57,143) increase compared with 2015. The commissariat managed government and internationally funded human rights and humanitarian assistance programs.

The CNDH, an independent ombudsman organization, includes government and civil society representatives. It actively monitored human rights conditions and advocated for government action to correct violations. Its annual budget was 105 million ouguiyas ($300,000). The CNDH produced an annual report on thematic topics, conducted regular investigations, and made recommendations to the government.

Section 6. Discrimination, Societal Abuses, and Trafficking in Persons

Women

<u>Rape and Domestic Violence</u>: Rape, including spousal rape, is illegal. Rapists who are single men face penalties of forced labor and whipping, and married rapists are subject to the death penalty. The government regularly enforced the law; 39 persons were convicted under the law and received various sentences. Nevertheless, as in years past, wealthy rape suspects reportedly avoided prosecution or, if prosecuted, avoided prison. Families of the victim commonly reached an agreement with the perpetrator for monetary compensation.

Local NGOs noted the incidence of both reported and unreported rape continued to be high, with the reported cases just a small fraction of the true total. National statistics on arrests and prosecutions for rape were unavailable, but the Association of Female Heads of Families (AFCF) reported 165 rapes between January and August, a marked decrease of 13 percent compared with 2015.

Between January and August, NGO Association for Health of Mother and Child reported 122 cases of registered rape in Nouakchott. Of these, 108 victims were minor girls, a net decrease compared with 159 cases reported in 2015.

Human rights activists and lawyers reported that rape victims were stigmatized, persecuted, and even imprisoned. Since rape is often associated with the concept of adultery, judges could, in theory, accuse the victim of fornication under sharia, hold the victim responsible for the rape, and imprison the victim. There were no reports this provision or interpretation of the law was enforced.

Domestic violence was also a serious problem. Spousal abuse and domestic violence are illegal, but there are no specific penalties for domestic violence. The government did not enforce the law effectively, and convictions were rare. Most cases went unreported. No reliable government statistics on prosecutions, convictions, and sentences for domestic violence were available. As of September the AFCF identified 1,225 cases of domestic violence (a 50 percent decrease compared with 2015).

Police and the judiciary occasionally intervened in domestic abuse cases, but women rarely sought legal redress, relying instead on family, NGOs, and community leaders to resolve domestic disputes. Traditional sharia judges handled many domestic violence cases. NGOs reported that, in certain cases, they asked police for help to protect victims of domestic violence, but police declined to investigate. The AFCF and other women's NGOs provided psychologists and shelter to some victims.

Female Genital Mutilation/Cutting (FGM/C): The law states that any act or attempt to damage a girl's sexual organs is punishable by imprisonment and a fine of 120,000 to 300,000 ouguiyas ($343 to $857). Nevertheless, authorities seldom applied the law, since the accompanying implementing law remained provisional.

FGM/C was practiced by all ethnic groups to varying degrees and performed on young girls, often on the seventh day after birth and almost always before the age of six months. Excision was the most severe form of FGM/C practiced. A 2013 UN Children's Fund (UNICEF) report estimated the prevalence among women at 69.4 percent, its prevalence among girls ages five to 18 at 54.8 percent, and its prevalence among girls under five at 46.6 percent.

During the year the government entered the third phase of the five-year FGM/C action plan, which aims to reinforce FGM/C policy and law, offer education and community support, encourage public declarations of FGM/C abandonment, and establish partnerships and public outreach campaigns. The government's program, which extends to 2017, focused on communities in the regions of Gorgol, Guidimaka, Hodh El Gharbi, Hodh El Chargui, Assaba, and Tagant. The program worked through five local NGOs to create association networks to conduct awareness campaigns against FGM/C.

During the year the government focused its efforts on the creation of the anti-FGM/C regional networks to denounce the practice of FGM/C; eight networks announced the abandonment of the practice.

The government, international organizations, and NGOs continued to coordinate their anti-FGM/C efforts, which focused on eradicating the practice in hospitals, discouraging midwives from performing FGM/C, and educating the population and elected officials on its dangers. The government, UN Population Fund (UNFPA), UNICEF, the National Imams' Association, and other members of civil society emphasized the serious health risks of FGM/C and sought to correct the widespread belief the practice was a religious requirement. The law prohibits government hospitals and licensed medical practitioners from performing FGM/C, and several government agencies worked to prevent others from perpetrating it. UNFPA had an agreement with the National School of Health to integrate FGM/C awareness into training curricula for midwives and nurses. According to several women's rights experts, these efforts appeared to be changing popular attitudes.

Other Harmful Traditional Practices: Traditional forms of mistreatment of women continued to decline. One of these is the forced feeding of adolescent girls prior to marriage, practiced by some Beydane families. Increased government, media, and civil society attention to the problem, including the health risks associated with excessive body weight, continued to lessen traditional encouragement of female obesity.

Sexual Harassment: There are no laws against sexual harassment. Women's NGOs reported that it was a common problem in the workplace.

Reproductive Rights: Couples and individuals have the right to decide the number, spacing, and timing of their children, and to manage their reproductive health, free from discrimination, coercion, or violence, but they often lacked the information to do so. Contraception was available at private health centers for those who could afford it. The UN Population Division estimated 12.5 percent of girls and women between the ages of 15 and 49 used a modern method of contraception in 2015.

The World Health Organization estimated the maternal mortality rate to be 602 per 100,000 live births, and a lifetime risk of maternal mortality of one in 36. The UNFPA estimated 21 percent of women ages 20-24 had given birth before the age of 18. The high maternal mortality rate was due to lack of medical equipment, low participation by mothers in programs promoting prenatal care, births without the assistance of health professionals, poor sanitary conditions during birth, maternal malnutrition, and high rates of adolescent pregnancy. According to UNICEF, skilled health personnel attended approximately 64.5 percent of births.

The AFCF stressed that these deficiencies applied in particular to poor women or to those from traditionally lower castes, such as slaves and former slaves, who often lacked access to contraception, obstetric and postpartum care, and treatment for sexually transmitted infections. The Mauritanian Association for the Health of Mothers and Children, which operated a center in Nouakchott for rape victims, provided emergency contraception to victims.

<u>Discrimination</u>: Women have legal rights to property and child custody, and the more educated and urbanized members of the population recognized these rights. Nevertheless, women had fewer legal rights than men. Divorced women, for example, could lose child custody if they remarried. According to common tradition, a woman's first marriage requires parental consent. The personal status code permits men to have up to four wives at the same time, but they are required to treat them equally. Government awareness programs encouraged women to obtain a contractual agreement at the time of marriage stipulating the marriage will end if the husband marries a second wife. This practice was common in Moor (Arab) society. Women who did not establish a solid contract remained unprotected. Moreover, government authorities did not always respect either the validity of such prenuptial agreements or the right to establish them. Polygyny continued to be relatively unusual among Moors, although its popularity has grown. The practice was more common among sub-Saharan ethnic groups. Arranged marriages were increasingly rare, particularly among the Moor population. Cultural resistance to intercaste marriage persisted. NGOs continued to report that powerful individuals used the judicial system to intimidate and persecute members of their families who married below their social rank.

Women faced other legal discrimination. According to sharia as applied in the country, the testimony of two women was necessary to equal that of one man. The courts granted only half as large an indemnity to the family of a female victim as that accorded to the family of a male victim. The personal status code provides a framework for the consistent application of secular law and sharia based family law, but judicial officials did not always respect it. Formulas for property distribution therefore varied widely from case to case. Human rights lawyers also reported judges treated differently cases concerning Beydane/Arab women, female slaves or low caste women, non-Arab citizen women, and foreign women.

Children

<u>Birth Registration</u>: By law a person generally derives citizenship from one's father. One can derive citizenship from one's mother under either of the following conditions: if the mother is a citizen and the father's nationality is unknown or he is stateless, or if the child was born in the country to a citizen mother and the child repudiates the father's nationality a year before reaching majority. Children born abroad to citizen mothers and foreign men can acquire citizenship one year before reaching the majority age of 18. Minor children of parents who have become naturalized citizens are also eligible for citizenship.

The process of registering a child and subsequently receiving a birth certificate is reportedly difficult. A lack of documentation, a situation common among the country's sub-Saharan ethnic minorities and the Haratines, may block a child's ability to enroll in school, travel, and have access to health care and other benefits of citizenship.

<u>Education</u>: The law mandates six years of school attendance for all children, but the law was not effectively enforced. Many children, particularly girls, did not attend school for six years. Children of slave caste Haratine families often did not receive any education.

<u>Child Abuse</u>: Child abuse occurred, but no data was available on its prevalence. As of September the AFCF identified 1,225 minor victims of domestic violence (a 50 percent decrease compared with 2015) and provided legal assistance to all of them.

<u>Early and Forced Marriage</u>: The legal marriage age is 18, but authorities rarely enforced the law, and child marriage was widespread. Since consensual sex outside of marriage is illegal, a legal guardian can ask local authorities to permit a girl younger than 18 to marry. Local authorities frequently granted permission. Nevertheless, the government continued to work with UNICEF to implement a program to combat child marriage through judicial and political reforms. It also cooperated with civil society to disseminate the personal status code, which sets the minimum age for marrying at 18 and requires a woman's consent to seal a union. These efforts appeared to show encouraging results. According to UNICEF in 2011 (the most recent data available), the percentage of children who were married before age 15 dropped from 19 to 15 percent, while the percentage of those married before age 18 fell from 43 to 35 percent.

<u>Female Genital Mutilation/Cutting (FGM/C)</u>: See information for girls under 18 in women's section above.

<u>Sexual Exploitation of Children</u>: The law prohibits sexual relations with a child under 18 years of age, with penalties of six months to two years in prison and a 120,000 to 180,000 ouguiyas ($343 to $514) fine. The possession of child pornography is illegal, with penalties of two months to one year in prison and a 160,000 to 300,000 ouguiyas ($457 to $857) fine. Commercial sexual exploitation of children is illegal, and conviction carries penalties of two to five years in prison and a fine of 200,000 to two million ouguiyas ($571 to $5,714). NGOs asserted the laws were not properly enforced.

<u>Displaced Children</u>: The Ministry of Social Affairs, Children, and Family identified 27,825 street children, but only monitored approximately 17,000, in nine of the country's 15 regions through youth integration centers and local NGOs. The centers focus on four major themes for the integration and promotion of children: enrollment in the civil register, social reintegration, fighting against child labor, and countering violence against children via psychosocial support. Despite this program, government assistance to these children was limited. A local NGO, Infancy and Development in Mauritania, monitored 227 children in Nouadhibou who lived on the streets largely as the result of poverty and the urbanization of formerly nomadic families.

<u>International Child Abductions</u>: The country is not a party to the 1980 Hague Convention on the Civil Aspects of International Child Abduction. See the Department of State's *Annual Report on International Parental Child Abduction* at travel.state.gov/content/childabduction/en/legal/compliance.html.

Anti-Semitism

A very small number of foreigners practiced Judaism. There were no reports of anti-Semitic acts.

Trafficking in Persons

See the Department of State's *Trafficking in Persons Report* at www.state.gov/j/tip/rls/tiprpt/.

Persons with Disabilities

The law prohibits discrimination against persons with physical, sensory, intellectual, and mental disabilities in employment, education, air travel and other transportation, access to healthcare, judicial system, or the provision of other state services. The law provides for access to information and communication, and to existing public buildings through retrofitting and future buildings through amendments to the building code. Authorities did not enforce the law, and persons with disabilities generally did not have access to buildings, information, and communications. The law provides for access to air transport and other transportation at reduced rates for persons with disabilities, although such access was often not available.

During the year the government maintained its annual disability assistance allocation of 85 million ouguiyas ($242,857) to 60 national associations and NGOs working on disabilities issues. As in the past, it also contributed 30 million ouguiyas ($86,000) in technical assistance. Unlike the previous year, the government mandated preference in government hiring to 100 persons with disabilities. The government hired nine full time employees with disabilities as of July, and 72 more persons with disabilities were in training and scheduled to begin work after completing training in December. Another 19 were in training to become labor inspectors in a training cycle that will end in 2017. The government also provided education and public accessibility for persons with disabilities, and some rehabilitation and other assistance through small income generating projects for such persons. One inspector from the Ministry of Social Affairs, Children, and Family was responsible for monitoring the projects' implementation and oversaw social reintegration programs for persons with disabilities. The ministry developed training programs and validated the certificates issued by the institutions created by professional associations of persons with disabilities. Persons with disabilities may file complaints with the ministry and seek additional recourse through the Court of Justice. During the year the ministry received no complaints, compared with only one the previous year.

On August 29, the Council of Ministers approved a draft law that mandates minimum architectural and technical conditions of access to public buildings for persons with disabilities. It also defines the technical and architectural requirements for access to communications, information, and public transport.

National/Racial/Ethnic Minorities

Some ethnic groups faced governmental discrimination while the Beydane (Arab) ethnic group received governmental preference. Western Saharan citizens of

Beydane (Arab) ethnicity often obtained national identity cards required for voting although they were not legally qualified to do so. Meanwhile, Haratine (Arab slave descendants) and sub-Saharan (non-Arab) citizens often had great difficulty obtaining national identity documents.

Racial and cultural tension and discrimination also arose from the geographic, linguistic, and cultural divides between "Moors" (Beydane and Haratine) who, while historically representing a mix of Berber, Arab and sub-Saharan Africans, today largely identify culturally and linguistically as Arab, and the sub-Saharan non-Arab minorities. The Moors encompass numerous tribal and clan groups and are further distinguished as either Beydane (White Moors) or Haratines (Black Moors, former slave caste). Beydane tribes and clans dominated positions in government and business far beyond their proportion of the population. The Haratines remained, as a group, politically and economically weaker than the Beydane, although they are the largest ethnocultural group in the country. The sub-Saharan ethnic groups, which included the Halpulaar (the largest non-Moor group), Soninke, and Wolof, were concentrated in the Senegal River Valley and urban areas. They, along with the Haratines, remained grossly underrepresented in leadership positions in government, industry, and the military (see section 3).

The constitution designates Arabic the official language and Arabic, Pulaar, Soninke, and Wolof as the country's national languages. The government continued to encourage French and Arabic bilingualism in the school system. Arabic is the armed forces' language of internal communication. Neither the sub-Saharan national languages nor the local Hassaniya Arabic dialect was used as a language of instruction.

Ethnic friction frequently underlay protests and incidents of labor unrest. On occasion, Haratine laborers invoked the legacy of slavery to explain their conflict with Beydane freight executives, port officials, retail store owners, and public safety officers.

Ethnic rivalry also contributed to political divisions and tensions. Some political parties tended to have readily identifiable ethnic bases, although political coalitions among parties were increasingly important. Haratines and persons of sub-Saharan origin remained underrepresented in mid- to high-level public and private sector jobs.

Reports of land disputes among Haratines, sub-Saharans, and Beydane were common. According to human rights activists and press reports, local authorities continued to allow Beydane to appropriate land occupied by Haratines and sub-Saharans, to occupy property unlawfully taken from sub-Saharans by former governments, and to obstruct access to water and pasturage. For example, in May, national political figures joined local human rights NGOs in accusing security forces of arresting and mistreating 14 sub-Saharan African women and three men in the village of Thiambene near Rosso following a land dispute related to a mango plantation.

As in years past, human rights NGOs reported numerous cases of inheritance disputes between slaves or former slaves and their masters. Traditionally, slave masters inherited their slaves' possessions.

Acts of Violence, Discrimination, and Other Abuses Based on Sexual Orientation and Gender Identity

No laws protect LGBTI persons from discrimination. Under sharia as applied in the country, consensual same-sex sexual activity between men is punishable by death if witnessed by four individuals, and such activity between women is punishable by three months to two years in prison and a fine of 5,000 to 60,000 ouguiyas ($14 to $171). The LGBTI community was rarely identified or discussed, which observers attributed to the severity of the stigma and legal penalties attached to such labels. No cases of abuses based on sexual orientation were reported during the year.

HIV and AIDS Social Stigma

Persons infected with HIV/AIDS were often isolated due to societal taboos and prejudice associated with the disease, but were gradually being accepted by society and the government. They were involved in the implementation of state programs to combat infectious diseases, HIV/AID, malaria, and tuberculosis.

Section 7. Worker Rights

a. Freedom of Association and the Right to Collective Bargaining

The law allows all workers, except members of police, armed forces, and foreign and migrant workers, to form and join independent unions of their choice at the local and national levels and provides for the right to conduct legal strikes and to bargain collectively.

Prior authorization or approval by authorities is required before a union may be recognized. The public prosecutor must authorize all trade unions before they enjoy legal status. The public prosecutor may provisionally suspend a trade union at the request of the Ministry of Interior and Decentralization if ministry officials believe the union has not complied with the law. The law also provides that authorities may initiate legal proceedings against union leaders who undermine public order or make false statements. This law, in effect, authorizes administrative authorities to dissolve, suspend, or deregister trade union organizations by unilateral decision. Noncitizens do not have the right to become trade union officials unless they have worked in the country and in the profession represented by the trade union for at least five years.

Bargaining collectively at the national level requires previous authorization or approval by the president, who decides how collective bargaining is organized. No such authorization is required for collective bargaining at the company level. The minister of labor, public service, and modernization of the administration may call for bargaining among employers, employees, labor unions, and the government. In addition, the ministry is entitled to take part in the preparation of collective agreements. The law provides that the meeting must occur 15 days following a statement of nonagreement between parties.

The law provides for the right to strike, but aggrieved parties must follow long and complex procedures before taking such action. The government may also dissolve a union for what it considers an illegal or politically motivated strike. The law prohibits workers from holding sit-ins or blocking nonstriking workers from entering work premises. Workers must provide advance notice of at least 10 working days to the Ministry of Labor, Public Service, and Modernization of the Administration for any strike.

The government did not enforce the law effectively, and resources and inspections were often inadequate. While authorities seldom punished violators, on several occasions the government ordered the reinstatement of workers who had been wrongfully terminated and/or directed companies to improve employee benefits and services. In November 2014 the president announced a salary increase of 50 percent for salaries of under 100,000 ouguiyas ($286) and a salary increase of 30 percent for salaries of more than 100,000 ouguiyas ($286) a year. This decision was implemented in January.

Freedom of association and the right to collective bargaining were not fully respected, although unions exercised their right to organize workers during the year. Collective bargaining at the company level, however, was rare. There were reports of government interference with union activities. According to the reports from the General Confederation of Mauritanian Workers, for instance, the Ministry of Fisheries and the Maritime Economy deducted overtime pay from workers who had engaged in trade union activities as a means of pressuring them to withdraw their union membership.

Registration and strike procedures were subject to lengthy delays and appeals. Labor ministry officials routinely issued notices calling on all parties to negotiate. Such notices legally restrict workers from striking for a period of four months. If negotiations fail to produce an agreement, the case is referred to the Court of Arbitration. If the court fails to broker a mutually satisfactory agreement, employees may have to wait up to four additional months from the time of the decision before they can legally strike.

Workers and unions organized several strikes, but in contrast with years past, authorities only occasionally employed force to disperse them.

While antiunion discrimination is illegal, national human rights groups and unions reported authorities did not actively investigate alleged antiunion practices in some private firms.

b. Prohibition of Forced or Compulsory Labor

The law prohibits all forms of forced or compulsory labor, including by children. It also criminalizes the practice of slavery and imposes penalties both on government officials who do not take action on reported cases and on those who benefit from contracting forced labor. The 2015 amendments to the law expand the definition of slavery to include forced labor and child labor. Although the government took some action toward ending slavery, such as the adoption of the Roadmap for the Eradication of the Vestiges of Slavery in 2014, its efforts to enforce the 2007 antislavery law were widely seen as inadequate, given the severity of the problem.

Tadamoun, the government agency charged with combating the "vestiges" of slavery, received 7.5 billion ouguiyas ($21.5 million) of public funding. Nevertheless, its progress continued to be slow, and evidence of programs directly reducing the "vestiges" of slavery was low. Throughout the year, Tadamoun's director general underscored his intention to address slavery through indirect means, such as awareness campaigns and local agriculture projects, rather than through referrals to criminal prosecutors.

Since December 2015 the country has opened two antislavery courts mandated by the 2015 amendments; however, the courts lacked funding and resources, and none of the appointed judges received training in how to deal with the unique challenges of investigating human trafficking cases, including how to prevent traffickers from intimidating victims and victims from withdrawing their cases. The first court was established in May in Nema, in the willaya (region) of Hodh El Gharbi in the southeast. The second was created in Nouakchott in July. A third opened in Nouadhibou but was not yet operational. On May 16, the court of Nema convicted and sentenced two men for slavery. The court sentenced Sidi Mohamed Ould Hanana and Hlehana Ould Hmeyada, who are cousins, to five years' imprisonment with one year to be served and four years suspended with supervision/probation, less than the maximum 10 years imprisonment allowed under the law. The court also imposed a fine of 100,000 ouguiyas ($285) and ordered payment of one million ouguiyas ($2,857) in restitution to each of the two female victims.

Immediately after Hanana's December 2015 arrest on these charges, his family reportedly entered a financial agreement with the family of his victim for 3,500,000 ouguiyas ($10,000). The amount was paid to the family, but did not stop the case from proceeding, as has routinely happened in previous cases. According to the court, Hmeyada's family, meanwhile, was also involved in the crime, but could not be prosecuted because they lived in Northern Mali, outside the court's jurisdiction.

Slavery-like practices, which typically flowed from ancestral master-slave relationships and involved both adults and children, continued throughout the year. Former slaves and their descendants remained in a dependent status in part due to a lack of marketable skills, poverty, and persistent drought. Such practices occurred primarily in areas where educational levels were generally low or a barter economy still prevailed, and in urban centers, including Nouakchott, where domestic servitude was relatively common. The practices commonly occurred where there was a need for workers to herd livestock, tend fields, and do other manual or household labor. Some former slaves and descendants of slaves were forced or had no other viable option than to work for their old masters in exchange for some combination of lodging, food, and medical care. Individuals in subservient circumstances were also vulnerable to mistreatment. Women with children faced particular difficulties; they could be compelled to remain in a condition of servitude, performing domestic duties, tending fields, or herding animals without remuneration.

Some former slaves reportedly continued to work for their former masters or others under exploitative conditions to retain access to land that they traditionally farmed. Although the law provides for distribution of land to the landless, including to former slaves, authorities rarely enforced it. Both NGO observers and government officials suggested that deeply embedded psychological and tribal bonds made it difficult for many individuals whose ancestors had been slaves for generations to break their bonds with former masters or their tribes. Some persons continued to link themselves to former masters because they believed their slave status had been divinely ordained or feared religious punishment if that bond was broken. Former slaves were often subjected to social discrimination and limited to performing manual labor in markets, ports, and airports.

Forced labor also occurred in urban centers where young children, often girls, were retained as unpaid household servants. Human rights groups reported that masters persuaded persons in slave-like relationships to deny such exploitative relationships to human rights activists.

NGOs continued to report cases of trafficking in persons for domestic service, street begging for unscrupulous religious teachers, and slave-like relationships as domestic servants or herders. Victims were men, women, and children.

In May the AFCF and El Hor (a leading antislavery NGO) denounced what they asserted was trafficking of young women from the Haratine community. The AFCF president stated that 300 young women, who initially went to Saudi Arabia to perform white collar employment, were instead used for menial labor and denied the right to terminate their employment. Local and international organizations helped repatriate 21 girls; others who wished to return home were in the process of repatriation. In its response to the complaints, the government characterized the actions of the Saudi employers in this case as allowable under a labor agreement between Mauritania and Saudi Arabia and stated the victims should file a legal complaint with the Ministry of Justice, which had an office for that purpose.

In December the *Meyadine* news website reported the government announced its decision to prevent any citizen woman from traveling to Saudi Arabia as a domestic worker. Specific instructions about the restriction were delivered to the authorities at Nouakchott International Airport.

Also see the Department of State's *Trafficking in Persons Report* at www.state.gov/j/tip/rls/tiprpt.

c. Prohibition of Child Labor and Minimum Age for Employment

The labor code sets the minimum age for employment at 14. Nevertheless, children as young as 12 may be employed in most forms of family enterprise with authorization from the Ministry of Labor, Public Service, and Modernization of the Administration, as long as the work does not affect the child's health, exceed two hours per day, or occurs during school hours or holidays. The law states employed children between ages 14 and 16 should receive 70 percent of the minimum wage and those who are 17 and 18 should receive 90 percent of the minimum wage. Children should not work more than eight hours a day and should be given one or several one-hour breaks, and may not work at night. In May the government began a participatory process that resulted in the development of a National Action Plan for the Elimination of Child Labor. This plan was an integral part of the government antislavery "Roadmap" adopted in 2014. The law prohibits employing or inciting a child to beg and provides penalties for violations ranging from one to eight months' imprisonment and a fine of 180,000 to 300,000 ouguiyas ($514 to $857). The penalties were generally insufficient to deter violations. The law does not prohibit hazardous occupations and activities in all relevant child labor sectors, including agriculture. Moreover, no law prohibits the use of children for illicit activities, such as the production and trafficking of drugs.

The government did not effectively enforce the law. According to a 2014 UNICEF report, 21.5 percent of children ages five to 14 were engaged in labor. Existing mechanisms for exchanging information among agencies or assessing effectiveness were not active during the reporting period. There was no specific mechanism for submitting complaints, other than to labor inspectors or the Special Police Brigade for Minors. NGOs were the only organizations that handled cases of child victims, referred them to the Special Police Brigade for Minors, and pressured the government to adjudicate the cases or integrate the victims in social centers or schools.

An unknown number of "talibes" (young students), nearly all from the Halpulaar community, begged in the streets and gave the proceeds to their religious teachers as payment for religious instruction. There were reliable reports some "marabouts" (religious teachers) forced their talibes to beg for more than 12 hours a day and provided them with insufficient food and shelter. The government continued a program to reduce the number of talibes and cooperated with NGOs to provide talibes with basic medical and nutritional care.

Child labor in the informal sector was common and a significant problem, particularly within poorer urban areas. Several reports suggested girls as young as seven, mainly from remote regions, were forced to work as unpaid domestic servants in wealthy urban homes.

Young children in the countryside were commonly engaged in cattle and goat herding, cultivation of subsistence crops, fishing, and other significant labor in support of their families. Young children in urban areas often drove donkey carts and delivered water and building materials. Street gang leaders forced children to steal, beg, and sell drugs in the streets of the capital. In keeping with longstanding tradition, many children also served apprenticeships in small industries, such as metalworking, carpentry, vehicle repair, masonry, and the informal sector. The government continued to operate seven Centers for Protection and Social Integration of Children in Difficult Situations: one each in Kiffa, Nouadhibou, Aleg, and Rosso, and three in Nouakchott. During the year, these centers hosted 370 children.

CNDH's 2016 annual report confirmed the extent of child labor, especially in rural areas. The report stated 26 percent of children between ages of 15 and 17 worked. The report indicated the proportion of children between ages of 12 and 14 who performed some work was up to 22 percent. The report also stressed the exploitation of girls was more frequent in domestic work.

Also see the Department of Labor's *Findings on the Worst Forms of Child Labor* at www.dol.gov/ilab/reports/child-labor/findings.

d. Discrimination with Respect to Employment and Occupation

Women faced legal discrimination in other areas (see section 6). The law prohibits discrimination based on race, disability, religion, political opinion, national origin, citizenship, social origin, sexual orientation and/or gender identity, age, or language, but the government often did not enforce the law. Discrimination in employment and occupation occurred with respect to race and language. For example, in conformity with long-standing practice, the advancement of both Haratines and sub-Saharans in the armed services remained limited.

The law provides that men and women should receive equal pay for equal work. The two largest employers, the civil service and the state mining company, observed this law; most employers in the private sector reportedly did not. In the modern wage sector, women also received family benefits, including three months of paid maternity leave.

e. Acceptable Conditions of Work

The nationally mandated minimum monthly wage for adults was 30,000 ouguiyas ($86). The most recent poverty level estimate by the government, from 2008, the latest year for which figures are available, was an annual income of 129,600 ouguiyas ($370), and the extreme poverty level for 2008 was an annual income of 96,400 ouguiyas ($275).

The law provides that the standard legal nonagricultural workweek must not exceed either 40 hours or six days, unless there is overtime compensation, which is to be paid at rates graduated according to the number of supplemental hours worked. Domestic workers and certain other categories could work 56 hours per week. The law provides that all employees must be given at least one 24-hour rest period per week. There are no legal provisions regarding compulsory overtime.

The Labor Office of the Ministry of Labor, Public Service, and Modernization of the Administration is responsible for enforcing labor laws but did not do so effectively. The country had 47 labor inspectors and 20 inspectors in training at the National School of Administration, who were expected to take up their positions in two years.

The government sets health and safety standards and in principle workers have the right to remove themselves from hazardous conditions without risking loss of employment. The law applies to all workers in the formal economy. The labor code applies to all workers regardless of nationality.

The majority of the working population labored in the informal sector, primarily in subsistence agriculture and animal husbandry. According to the General Confederation of Workers of Mauritania, only 25 percent of workers filled positions with regular pay.

Despite the law, labor unions pointed to conditions approaching modern slavery in several sectors, including the food processing industry. In these sectors, workers did not have contracts or receive pay stubs. Their salaries were below the official minimum wage, and they worked in unfavorable conditions. Sometimes they did not receive pay for several months.

Working conditions in the fishing industry were similarly difficult. Commercial fishermen reportedly often exceeded 40 hours of work per week without receiving overtime pay. Additionally, some factory workers employed by fish processing plants and boat manufacturers did not receive contracts guaranteeing the terms of their employment. Government inspections of fishing vessels, processing plants, and boat factories remained rare.

Violations of minimum wage or overtime laws were frequent in many sectors but more common in the informal economy, which includes domestic service, street vending, artisanal fishing, garbage collection, bus fare collection, donkey cart driving, apprenticeship, auto repair, and other employment.

According to the General Confederation of Workers of Mauritania, the National Agency of Social Security registered 181 workplace fatalities or injuries through December, 89 of which occurred at National Industrial and Mining Company, the national mining company. There was a substantial net decrease of 236 cases of workplace fatalities as compared with 417 fatalities in 2015.